Beautiful America's

Idaho

Front Cover, Red Fish Lake, Sawtooth N.R.A.

Published by Beautiful America Publishing Company®
9725 S.W. Commerce Circle
Wilsonville, Oregon 97070

Library of Congress Cataloging-in-Publication Data
Beautiful America's Idaho
1. Idaho — Description and travel — Views.   I. Title.
F747.S74   1989   917.96—dc20   89-15058
ISBN 0-89802-537-0
ISBN 0-89802-536-2 (Paperback)

Idaho State Capitol, Boise

Beautiful America's

Idaho

Text by
Linda Sterling-Wanner

Contents

Introduction

America the Beautiful could have been written for the state of Idaho. Only the words "from sea to shining sea" do not apply and even then Idaho has an inland seaport where ships travel 470 miles from the ocean to the city of Lewiston to dock. If you hum the words to yourself, as you travel through this volume you'll experience the majestic mountains, the fertile plains, the great spaces.

In space alone, Idaho is grand. Its acreage is about the size of Great Britain including England, Scotland and Wales. In the eyes of this beholder, Idaho's greatest feature lies in the diversity of her terrain. Her mountains rise to 12,662 feet and her lowest elevation is 738 feet. Over forty peaks touch sky at more than 10,000 feet and Hell's Canyon trenches through Idaho rock and soil to claim the distinction as the deepest gorge on the North American Continent.

Idaho holds other distinctions as well. Shoshone Falls, on the Snake River near Twin Falls, plunges over a basalt horseshoe rim nearly a thousand feet wide, dropping two hundred and twelve feet—a depth greater than famous Niagara Falls.

Scenic diversity is enormous throughout the state. The whitewater cascades of the Salmon and Snake Rivers; the golden plains of the Palouse Range; the Bruneau Dunes, tallest sand dunes in America; the sculpted granite of Balanced Rock; the mineral waters of Lava Hot Springs; crystal-holding caves; geysers; underground rivers; and so, so much more—are

St. Joe River near St. Maries

(Opposite) Harrison Peak in Selkirk Crest, Kaniksu National Forest

all yours to explore and enjoy.

Discover, too, Idaho's gemfields. Idaho produces seventy-two kinds of precious and semi-precious stones—her gem beds are second only to those of Africa. And gold—the lure that brought many early settlers—can still be found in almost every county in Idaho.

One of the fastest growing areas in the country, Idaho nevertheless remains uncrowded with an average of just over twelve persons per square mile. The people of Idaho are a friendly bunch, eager to share the bounty of their region. When you stop in for a burger and slice of pie at a roadside cafe, you're likely to get the cook's recipe for lemon meringue and the fellow at the counter will offer directions to his favorite fishing spot.

Her welcoming citizens, her scenic beauty and abundant wildlife, the festivals and activities and many historical attractions, make Idaho a place to visit again and again. She is America at her finest—Idaho the Beautiful.

Linda Sterling-Wanner

North Idaho

Whether a waterside luxury hotel is your accommodation of choice or an island campsite is more your style, you'll find the perfect location in the Panhandle, as Northern Idaho is called. It isn't by accident that mentioning places to stay in Northern Idaho usually includes a spot by a river or lake. No greater concentration of lakes can be found in any other Western state.

The lakes and rivers are part of the attraction, but one must add to them the enhancing background created by the dramatic Bitterroot, Selkirk, and Cabinet Mountains. Their ridges hold pristine lakes filled with brook trout for anglers, or you can venture into the forests simply to indulge in sweet-tasting wild huckleberries or to smell the warm richness of the timber. Northern Idaho's wild, unspoiled forests are home to abundant wildlife including moose, elk, deer, bear, mountain caribou, cougar, lynx, bighorn sheep, mountain goat, bobcat, coyote and other animals.

There are many trails for hiking, whether it is for a few hours walk or for a week-long backpacking expedition into the mountains. Near Priest Lake, Hanna Flats Nature Trail and the route to the Roosevelt Grove of Ancient Cedars offer easy hiking. Seeing the ancient cedars is something special, for the grove has trees up to twelve feet in diameter and 150 feet tall. Round Lake and Farragut State Park also offer a variety of scenic hiking paths.

To obtain a view without a hike, the Schweitzer chair lift is open in the summer. A ride

Cataldo Mission, Cataldo

Coeur D'Alene Lake at sunset

to the top affords a sweeping vista of Lake Pend Oreille and the Selkirk and Cabinet Mountains.

It seems when Idahoans aren't out hiking they are fishing. The high mountain lakes provide brook trout for hike-in anglers. The North Fork and the Little North Fork of the Coeur d'Alene River offer good fly fishing, too.

If you want to leave the fishing to the eagles, you can choose to view the water by every kind of craft from canoes to sailboats. Marinas on Coeur d'Alene, Pend Oreille and Priest lakes have boats for rent, or if you bring your own boat you will find plenty of launching ramps.

Pend Oreille is known for its favorable sailing winds and weekends often include sailing events. Pend Oreille is the biggest of the lakes and one of the largest in the West, with a shoreline of more than 111 miles. Farragut State Park, south of Sandpoint, offers thousands of acres of open space and campsites on the lake.

A different and charming boating vacation can be had at Upper Priest Lake. Priest Lake is ringed by dense forest and studded with small islands where remote boat-only campsites can be found. Several rustic resorts are tucked beneath the trees and offer relaxed vacations focused on water sports. Priest is connected to Upper Priest by a waterway called the Thoroughfare, a narrow tree-lined corridor popular with canoeists. Hiking trails wind from both Priest and Upper Priest into the Selkirk Mountains. In the winter both lakes freeze over and are used for snowmobiling and cross-country skiing.

If you're not handy with a boat, let someone else do the driving. Sightseeing cruises can be booked out of Coeur d'Alene from late May through September. A paddlewheeler excursion runs on the Kootenai River from Bonners Ferry during the summer months, or group tours are available by appointment on Lake Pend Oreille from the cities of Hope and Sandpoint.

Though it sometimes seems as though Northern Idaho is a land owned solely by nature and her creatures, there are cities tucked into the eye-catching settings and these cities and towns are as charming and varied as the landscape itself.

Bonners Ferry, located in Boundary County, is touted as "the last frontier in the contiguous U.S.A." Bordering Canada and Montana, the county is the scenic route to Glacier National Park. Outside of Bonners Ferry on U.S. Highway 2 is the Moyie Bridge, a 1,223 foot bridge hovering between canyon walls and suspended 450 feet over white water rapids. Adding to the attraction are the Moyie Falls, just west of the bridge. They plummet to earth in a fusillade of white thunder and spraying mist, creating one of Northern Idaho's most breathtaking sights.

Around Bonners Ferry, the American Bald Eagle, sturgeon, and other threatened or endangered species can still be found. The human species makes Bonners Ferry a recreational focal point. Because the town straddles the Kootenai River it makes an ideal base for river fishing expeditions. The area is a natural start for hiking or horsepacking trips into the surrounding mountains or for snowmobiling in the wintertime. During the summer months, a sternwheel excursion boat operates on the Kootenai River and rafting companies run trips down the Moyie River.

Most of the activity surrounding Pend Oreille is centered in Sandpoint. Sandpoint is known for its sandy beaches, small resorts and marinas, and the community's devotion to culture. The city is also noted for having the nation's first marketplace on a bridge. This bridge, known as the Cedar Street Bridge, was raved about in the *Wall Street Journal*, *Americana*, and the *Los Angeles Times*. It spans a picturesque creek and sits within the protective enclave of the Selkirk Mountains. A walk on the Bridge brings surroundings of sunlight, greenery, delectible cooking smells, and the colorful array of vendor's carts.

From spring through fall the focus in Sandpoint is on water recreation—fishing, sailing, water skiing and sunbathing on the beach. In winter, Sandpoint becomes headquarters for snowmobilers, ice fishermen and cross-country skiers. Schweitzer, the leading ski resort

(Opposite) Palouse farm country

Harvest time near Worley

in the Northern Rockies, is just outside of town. Ski conditions at Schweitzer are so consistently good that the management guarantees them—something no other ski area in the U.S. is willing to do.

Outside Sandpoint on U.S. 95 is Farragut State Park. In addition to superb camping, visitors can see old navy photographs and natural history exhibits at a museum located in the park, for Farragut was once the second largest U.S. naval training center. Franklin Roosevelt chose the site during World War II for submarine testing because the bottom of Lake Pend Oreille is an incredible 1,225 feet deep. Today, near the town of Bayview, the navy still uses Lake Pend Oreille to test small, electronically controlled submarines, but at Farragut there is only solitude among pine and lush fern.

When North Idahoans boast about their area of the state the city of Coeur d'Alene is often mentioned. *U.S. News and World Report* named it one of the ten best cities in America in which to live. *National Geographic* has described the lake as "one of the five most beautiful in the world."

If you visit Coeur d'Alene, Sandpoint, Bonners Ferry or one of the many smaller towns you'll discover why the hospitality and the scenery combine to make Northern Idaho one of America's finest areas.

Pioneer Mountain

North Central Idaho

In common with the northern portion of the state, North Central Idaho seems at first glance to be a land of water and wilderness minus civilization. What has actually happened is the people of this area have managed to keep the fresh appeal of the land, living their lives in harmony with the beauty that surrounds them...and that beauty is enormous in more than one sense!

Much of North Central Idaho is consumed by one of the largest designated wilderness areas in the lower 48 states— the Selway Bitterroot Wilderness, the Gospel Hump Wilderness and the Frank Church River of No Return Wilderness Area. Many lands designated "primitive areas" are also to be found in this section of Idaho, including the Mallard-Larkins Pioneer Area.

The rivers claiming this land flow deep, thundering between narrow canyons or suddenly widening to provide great pools of blue-green reflection. Whitetail deer and elk abound along the banks and the water glistens with flashes of color from the backs of steelhead, kokanee and wild trout. Even at the liveliest time, summer, when backpacking, horseback riding, hiking, and river floating are favored activities, the rivers are uncrowded. It's easy to close your eyes and listen to the wind in pine and aspen and allow it to wrap you in its special kind of silence; open your eyes to the unbridled ruggedness and you'll feel like those first explorers must have felt when they entered Idaho.

If you want to take that feeling one step further, travel Highway 12 to the Lochsa River where the roadway parallels the route of the Lewis and Clark expedition. Lewis and Clark, under President Thomas Jefferson's commission, were guided over the Bitterroot range into Idaho by Sacajawea...the Shoshone wife of Charbonneau, a French fur trapper.

Sacajewea's Idaho remains as charismatic today as when she led the expedition; the change is primarily in accessibility and sometimes even that accessibility is still limited.

For instance, only a few rough roads lead into the world famous Hell's Canyon. A better route for viewing the deepest chasm in North America can be had by jet boating up the river. Charter trips can be booked from the city of Lewiston.

The Oxbow, Brownlee, and Hells Canyon Dams are all easily accessible. Over 19,000 acres of water skiing, boating and excellent fishing along with the availability of float and jet boat trips draw tourists and natives alike to these popular areas.

An opposite to the canyon depths of Oxbow, Brownlee and Hell's Canyon are the cloud-touching peaks of the Seven Devils Scenic Area. The seven peaks lurch upward from the Snake River to a breath-gasping 9,000 feet. Around the peaks of the Seven Devils you may be lucky enough to see a fluffy white Rocky Mountain Goat. Somewhat easier to spot are thirty alpine lakes. They don't require mountain goat climbing abilities, but you do have to hike or backpack to them. To start your trip, take the gravel road on the right one mile south of Riggins and continue on to Windy Saddle Camp and hike from there. Those who don't care to hike yet cherish a beautiful view can continue on two miles above Windy Saddle Camp for a view at Heaven's Gate. Appropriately named, this spot at the top of the world provides a panorama of Washington, Oregon, Montana and Idaho.

Closer to earth, the Rapid River Fish Hatchery near the town of Riggins makes an interesting stop. Rapid River is one of the Northwest's most prolific chinook salmon hatcheries. The town of Riggins itself is the area's white water capital. A number of outfitters offer rubber raft excursions or jet boat trips down the Salmon River. The Salmon River

Soldier Mountains near Camas Prairie

(Opposite) Lochsa River, Clearwater National Forest

is one of the most spectacular, dramatic rivers in the world. A float trip on the Salmon takes you past abandoned mines, old Indian burial grounds and fishing camps, and enchants you with sightings of ancient Indian petroglyphs. Elk, deer, goats and dozens of bird species come down to the river. Arrangements for river trips, or for a stay at one of Idaho's fine guest ranches, can usually be made at Riggins or through the Idaho Outfitters and Guides. Two other challenging whitewater rivers are the Lochsa and Selway.

Plan your float trips ahead of time. Many of the rivers require permits if your adventure isn't scheduled with an outfitter. A limited number of permits are available each season and they must be procured several months in advance.

North of Riggins the Clearwater and Snake River converge near the city of Lewiston. Amazingly, Lewiston serves as an inland seaport. Ships travel 470 miles from the ocean, up the Columbia and Snake Rivers, to dock in Lewiston.

The scenery around the Lewiston/Moscow area is quite different from the middle portion of North Central Idaho. Here, sharp crags and great depths have been transformed into rolling hills.

An interesting day-trip can be had by taking the Camas Prairie-Grangeville route out of Lewiston. Historical sites, vivid scenery, and friendly people will make your trip a delight. If you take Highway 95 south, you'll pass the Potlatch mill and paper plant and enter the Nez Perce National Historical Park and Tribal Headquarters. At Spaulding, you can tour the Nez Perce National Historical Park Museum to see an excellent collection of Nez Perce artifacts. While in the rich Nez Perce homeland, visit the ruins of an 1861 Indian Agency, tour a Presbyterian church built in the mid-1880s, and see Poor Coyote cabin.

Continuing on down the road, you'll pass the famous Camas Prairie Railroad (with 64 trestles in 85 miles); Winchester State Park; the Benedictine Sisters Convent and Museum near Cottonwood; Weis Rockshelter (5500 BC); the Camas Prairie (named for the camas plant, an Indian food); and end up at Grangeville—a smokejumpers' base, home to the

Ray Holes Saddle Company, and a jumping off place for the Idaho wilderness.

Idaho's oldest university, the University of Idaho, is located north of Grangeville in Moscow. Established in 1887 by the Idaho Territorial Legislature, the 450 acre University of Idaho campus holds Gothic structures and unique modern complexes like the Kibbie Dome with its 150 foot wooden arches. Moscow and quality cultural activities are synonymous. Moscow residents take pride in the fact that their community supports and encourages a creative atmosphere where artisans can practice and perfect their crafts. The city is home to the American Festival Ballet and the Idaho Repertory Theatre. Major college sports, celebrity events, and music festivals offer further activities.

Outside Moscow the Palouse Range stretches in a waving farmland quilt of golden wheat, green lentils and peas—interspersed with patches of rich brown soil. Red barns and farmhouses occasionally add their dollop of color to the pastoral scenery.

If you seek natural beauty and friendly people, the diverse area of North Central Idaho will not disappoint you.

Fall River near Rexburg

McCall Harbor, Payette Lake

McCall Ice Sculpture

Southwestern Idaho

Southwestern Idaho, sculpted into rugged mountains, brushed into golden desert, or heady with the scent of apple blossoms, is a land of infinite variety.

The upper portion of this section cradles the small towns of New Meadows, McCall, Council and Cascade in postcard-like settings. The towns are framed by mountain peaks and alpine lakes are sprinkled throughout the mountains in every direction.

The city of McCall sits on the southern shore of azure Payette Lake. This placid lake was created ten to twenty-five thousand years ago by a valley glacier. Its sparkling waters are dotted in summertime with the bright reds, blues and yellows of sailing regattas. In winter the town is nestled in some of the deepest snows in the west. Brundage Mountain ski area, just seven miles north of McCall, has helped the town earn its name "Ski Town USA." Representatives from McCall have been sent to all but four winter olympics. Another attraction is the McCall Winter Carnival. People travel from all over the nation to see the towering ice sculptures local residents and national artisans mold. McCall can truly be said to be a town with year-round charm.

The Payette River Scenic Route out of McCall winds past the town of Cascade. The town sits on the dam site on the southwest side of Cascade Lake. The reservoir created by the dam attracts nearly 300,000 visitors a year. Pleasant days can be spent picnicking, hiking, camping, waterskiing, horseback riding or simply relaxing around one of the many campgrounds. The lake is said to be the number one fishing lake in Idaho. Wintertime expands the lake-oriented activities to include snow-mobiling, ice-fishing, and cross-country skiing.

The secluded Warm Lake recreation area lies just twenty miles east of Cascade on the edge of Idaho's wilderness area. Rent a rustic cabin or stay at one of the campgrounds to enjoy this pristine outdoor setting.

Cambridge, southwest of Cascade and McCall, is the southern gateway to Hell's Canyon. This small town has an authentic display of a working blacksmith shop, a settler's cabin, a one-room school house and flour and saw mills.

About twenty miles south of Cambridge lies the city of Weiser, known as the home of the National Oldtime Fiddlers' Contest. Every June, foot-stomping hoedowns bring outstanding fiddlers of all ages from across the country. You can attend the competition and enjoy the playoffs or wander the streets and campgrounds to listen to impromptu melodies.

Other festivals of note in nearby towns are the Apple Blossom Festival in Payette, Horseshoe Days in New Plymouth and the Cherry Festival in Emmett. All are "join in the fun" festivals that extend a welcome to natives and visitors alike.

That "open-arms" policy radiates throughout the area. Another commonality these communities share is the farming tradition. Fertile soil, abundant irrigation water and a relatively mild climate (about a 160-day growing season of constant sunshine) make possible the production of dozens of crop varieties. The Western Treasure Valley, which includes Weiser, Payette, Fruitland and New Plymouth, grows more acres of sugar beets, onions and alfalfa seed than any other region in the country. Corn, potatoes, flower seed, hay and grain are also grown. Parma is a major seed production area and the Fruitland area leads the counties of Idaho in the production of apples, prunes and plums.

For an agricultural tour, travel to Caldwell, Idaho. A fifty mile drive-it-yourself excursion

South Fork Boise River

(Opposite) Dry Creek and Lost River Range

covering a varied agricultural area, including three of Idaho's wineries, makes a pleasant way to spend an afternoon. The city offers tour maps. Known as Canyon County, this section of Idaho contributes 80% of the nation's supply of hybrid sweet corn seed. When you drive around the Caldwell/Nampa area, it's hard to imagine these thriving towns with their outlying high-yielding farms were once only an oasis in a desert of sagebrush and ankle-deep alkali dust.

While traveling through, you may enjoy the Givens Hot Springs, a natural hot springs twenty miles south of Caldwell.

Sixty miles south of Caldwell you'll discover Silver City. A famous mining town in the 1860's, it is one of Idaho's most picturesque ghost towns.

Another ghost town comes alive by taking a short drive from Boise. Idaho City loomed as the largest town in the Northwest back in 1865. A rip-roaring mining camp, it was the center of one of the richest gold strikes in North America. The town is a well-preserved relic of bustling, brawling boomtown days. Idaho's oldest store, the Boise Basin Mercantile, and several saloons and restaurants are open for business. The Idaho City Hotel rents antique rooms. You can peek inside the Territorial Jail or walk among the graves at Boot Hill Cemetary. If you decide to walk about the hills that contain some of the old mining areas you may come across one of the early Chinese "homes." A few of the Chinese who surged into the area to seek their fortune were able to build hurridly constructed shacks, but many poorer Chinese dug crude homes in the ground. Some of these seemingly child-size trenches, with only a board for a pallet-bed and another board for a shelf on which to set a small cookstove, can still be found.

Away from the nostalgia of Idaho City, Idaho's capital city of Boise picks up the pace. There's so much to see and do around Boise it's almost impossible to capture it all. Highlights are trips to the Morrison Center for the Performing Arts; Julia Davis Park, which is home to the Boise City Zoo; the Boise Art Museum; the Idaho Historical Museum; the Old Idaho

Penitentiary with its Botanical Gardens; the annual Idaho Shakespeare Festival; and Ann Morrison Park.

Mountain Home completes the tour of Southwestern Idaho. About an hours drive southeast of Boise, the community of Mountain Home revolves around the Mountain Home Air Force Base where each September there's an air show. At other times you may see F111A and EF-111A Raven fighter squadrons racing across the sky in training sessions.

South of Mountain Home off Highway 51 a slice of desert crowds against the Snake River. The Bruneau Dunes State Park contain (if the shifting sand can be said to be contained!) the tallest sand dunes in America.

Mountains, farmlands, sand dunes—where else but Southwestern Idaho?

Bruneau River Canyon

South Central Idaho

In the upper corner of South Central Idaho lie Ketchum and Sun Valley. Residents confess they came for the world-famous winter skiing, but moved there for the terrific summers. These towns at the foot of the Sawtooth Recreational Area hold an inherent surplus of scenic and recreational activities. By raft or kayak you can tackle popular white water spots, or fish for steelhead and trout in one of the streams that lure flycasters from all over. On a bright summer day you can ice skate on the country's only outdoor rink. Tennis buffs can volley on eighty-five different uncrowded courts. Golf enthusiasts have a choice of four alpine courses.

Another popular summer activity is a countryside bicycle tour. You can rent a mountain bike at a Sun Valley shop to cycle the roads of Wood River or take a back country hiking trail. A different way of seeing the woodlands is by horseback. Valley stables offer tours and for those new to riding, the opportunity for lessons in English or Western riding.

While you're scouting the countryside don't miss the breathtaking views along Trail Creek. The Ernest Hemingway Memorial on Trail Creek pays tribute to the Nobel Prize-winning author who spent his last years in the valley and is buried in the Ketchum cemetary.

Winter is, of course, the season for which Sun Valley is acclaimed. Sun Valley's reputation evolved quickly when handsome railroad executive Averell Harriman stepped into the picture. It was the 1930's and Harriman, impressed with the Winter Olympics at Lake Placid,

Sunset on the Boise River

Bruneau Dunes State Park

New York, sought the assistance of Austrian Count Felix Schaffgotsch to find a site in the West comparable to the Swiss and Austrian Alps. Soon the world-class mountains and European villages of Sun Valley drew tourists and celebrities eager to try the latest rage . . . skiing! Adventurers like Gary Cooper, Ingrid Bergman and Clark Gable were followed by Ernest Hemingway and Marilyn Monroe. The world's first chairlifts brought even more celebrities and tourists. Today the challenging slopes, blue skies, and the spectacular scenery of this protected valley continue to issue invitation as one of Idaho's greatest attractions.

The pine-scented country north of Ketchum is known as the Sawtooth National Recreation Area. Public campgrounds allow you to pitch a tent, or secluded guest ranches, motels and resorts offer accomodations for tourists less "primitive." Either way, the snowy peaks and sparkling waters demand attention. You can hike, fish, trail ride, or boat in the summer and come back for snowmobiling and nordic skiing during wintertime.

When you enter the park through the Sawtooth National Recreation Area Headquarters, a friendly ranger will provide you with a cassette player and tape with a descriptive commentary of the sites you'll pass as you drive through the Sawtooth National Recreation Area wilderness. At the northern end of the highway you simply return the tape to the Stanley Ranger Station.

Near the town of Stanley over three million chinook salmon are raised each year at the Sawtooth National Fish Hatchery.

On the same highway that takes you into the Sawtooths, go south instead of north and you'll come across two of the natural wonders of the world, the Shoshone Ice Cave and Mammoth Cave. Shoshone is a lava tube that stretches to the equivalent of three city blocks. Glittering ice crystals sparkle everywhere. Outside the cave prehistoric animal fossils that were discovered in the cave are on display. No wonder *Sunset Magazine* rated Shoshone Cave as one of the main points of interest in the Northwest.

Nearby Mammoth Cave, though it is less glamorous, is nonetheless fascinating in that a trip into the mile-deep cavern provides a view of formations from early volcanic explosions.

Continuing down Idaho 75 you'll arrive at Twin Falls. In 1904 Twin Falls was the source of what was the most massive undertaking in history at that time—turning desert wasteland into farmland by diverting the waters of the Snake River into miles of irrigation canals. The project created what's known today as one of the most productive farm areas in the country—Magic Valley.

The city of Twin Falls perches on the edge of the mesmerizing Snake River Canyon. The many falls and great drops of sheer walls make for powerful scenery. Especially notable is Shoshone Falls, the "Niagara of the West." Its foaming waters plunge over 200 feet down, filling the air with a dancing multicolored mist. Another "not to be missed" sight is the 1500 foot long Perrine Bridge. Towering 486 feet above the Snake River, it is near the site where Evel Knievel attempted to jump the river in a rocket cycle. Back in Twin Falls, the Heritage Museum houses many interesting exhibits including relics of the Great Basin Shoshone-Bannock tribes and of the cliff-dwelling Anasazi.

A stop at the town of Burley in late June will place you in the midst of one of the six nationally recognized speedboat regattas. South of Burley a dirt road enters the Silent City of Rocks. The route is the same one the early pioneers took as they headed down the Oregon portion of the California trail. Five hundred acres of granite rocks make eerie surroundings, particularly since many of the monoliths loom up to 60 stories in height. A number of the broad rocks hold pioneer inscriptions written in axle grease upon their faces. Maybe you'll be the lucky one who comes across the Almo gold stolen in 1878 from an Overland Stage. It is said that one of the robbers, upon his deathbed, confessed to burying the gold near the Silent City of Rocks.

Traveling further along this route you'll drive through historic Oakley, where pioneer homes with wrap-around porches and elegant construction sit in slightly-faded splendor. Stop at the Daughters of the Pioneers Museum or visit the cemetary with its white marble

The Falls at Thousand Springs near Gooding

Snake River Canyon near Twin Falls

tombstones and let your imagination take over where history leads off.

The Pomerelle Ski Area is close by as are the Mormon Reservoir and Magic Reservoir. Waterskiing, windsurfing, sailing, and fishing for 10-12 pound Brown trout are favorite reservoir-based activities. In winter the famous Idaho snow expands the seasons of fun in South Central Idaho.

Southeastern Idaho

Southeastern Idaho is an area of bright livability tucked into a corner of Idaho that is a mixture of streams, valleys, lava canyons and more.

Following the wagon ruts worn into the soil by other pioneers, the Mormon settlers moved across Idaho establishing farms and ranches. The small towns and countryside of Southeastern Idaho are rich with the history of these and other travelers and settlers in the Old West.

The city of Blackfoot inhabits the upper corner of this section. Blackfoot is an appealing stop-over point only a few hours from Salt Lake City and is just down river from Yellowstone and Grand Teton National Park. A lot of Native American Indians can be seen in and around Blackfoot because the Fort Hall Indian Reservation is directly south of the city. The four-day Shoshone-Bannock Indian Festival at Fort Hall in mid-August features a colorful war dance competition, Indian games and an art exhibit.

During a visit to Blackfoot, golf enthusiasts shouldn't miss the Blackfoot Municipal Course. Considered one of the best courses in Idaho, the greens rating of 71.4 make it one of the toughest, too. After a good golf game a picnic at Jensen's Grove, a man-made lake near the Snake River, might be just the ticket. Closer to town, the aluminum geodesic dome of the Municipal Pool holds six competition lanes, a diving well and a children's pool.

Further away, the city of Pocatello, once the largest rail center west of the Mississippi,

Scenic Silver Creek near Gannett

Alice Lake in the Sawtooth Mountains

is a railroad buff's treat. The towering, elaborate three-story structure of the Oregon Short Line Depot was designed at the turn of the century. The lovely Yellowstone Hotel across the street provided overnight lodging for train passengers. To further increase your knowledge of the trains and of the Pocatello countryside, stop by the Bannock County Historical Museum. Pioneer and Indian relics can be seen at the Idaho Museum of Natural History on the Idaho State University campus.

The Oregon Trail led through Pocatello, its travelers stopping at Fort Hall. A full-scale replica of the famous fort has been built, exact in details pulled from original Hudson Bay Company plans. Settings inside the fort are duplicated, too, with shops like the Depot Drugstore and the Wood River Restaurant and Saloon.

A fascinating geological and historical area west of Pocatello and only twelve miles west of the city of American Falls, is Massacre Rocks State Park. Devil's Gate Pass, which is the narrow pass through which the Oregon Trail traveled, is all that remains of an extinct volcano. Immigrants following the Oregon Trail called this area "Gate of Death" and "Devil's Gate." The pioneers feared the "hostiles" that might lay waiting to ambush their caravans. Register Rock, within the park, was a rest stop for the weary travelers. Register Rock derives its name from the many names inscribed by the immigrants.

Massacre Rocks has become a favorite area for bird watchers. Over 200 species of birds have been sighted within the park. Whistling swans, blue herons, and bald eagles are common. The desert environment is also home to rabbits, coyotes, muskrats and beaver.

Using the same skills she used in forming Massacre Rocks, Mother Nature left tantalizing traces of her power in Minnetonka Cave and the Crystal Ice Caves (both are a short drive from American Falls). Minnetonka's half-mile depths open to rooms of glittering ice crystal and banded travertine rock. Prehistoric plant and marine animal fossils are among the stalactites and stalagmites.

Ancient volcanic activity at the Great Rift National Landmark formed a crater of 100 feet across and 150 feet in depth. Inside the crater lie the Crystal Ice Caves. Descending 155 feet into the caves, you'll discover a lake of ice with stalagmites reaching up to sixteen feet in height.

Off Interstate 15, discover Lava Hot Springs. Centuries ago, Indians used the Lava Hot Springs for curative and recreational purposes. Modern visitors to the town of Lava Hot Springs can swim in a million gallons of 86 degree water in a free form Olympic-size pool or its AAU size companion (nearly a third-of-an-acre) — or soak in the pleasurably hot (110 degree) mineral waters the town took its name from.

Portneuf River is a premier trout stream that flows through Lava Hot Springs. A crop of youngsters is usually on it in summertime, squealing with delight as they tube through town.

A Tosoiba water geyser shoots over 100 feet into the air in the town of Soda Springs. The 175 foot high carbon dioxide gas geyser is the largest of its kind in the world. The city has "contained" the geyser so it is set to go off hourly, "except," say residents, "when the wind is from the west and would blow it over the business district of town."

Five large parks around Soda Springs make pleasant living, and close reservoirs provide boating, water skiing, and speedboat racing. Cross-country skiing, snowmobiling and ice-fishing also claim residents' time.

To see the history of Idaho unfurled take a road trip through the towns of Montpelier, Malad, Franklin, Preston, and Paris. Historic churches and homes and other sites of interest are plentiful. Preston is an especially charming little town with a natural mineral springs resort. Its past is notorious in that it was the site of the Bear River Massacre, one of the bloodiest Indian massacres in history. Franklin, the first white settlement in Idaho, holds the title of oldest town in Idaho.

A perfect finale to a trip around Southeastern Idaho might end with a stop at Bear Lake. A turquoise-colored high mountain refuge, Bear Lake is shared by Idaho and Utah. The

Bald Mountain at Sun Valley

Sun Valley

Sun Valley Inn

lake is a four-season vacation mecca that remains unhurried and unspoiled. Limitless mountain trails in the Bear Lake Recreation Area lead to unspoiled beauty and solitude. One of these trails may lead to Peg-Leg's gold, buried somewhere east of Bear Lake in the grave of his Indian wife.

The north end of Bear Lake belongs to the Bear Lake National Wildlife Refuge. Echos of bird-song and bird-calls reverberate across the 17,600 acre marsh.

All activities lead back to Bear Lake and its beautiful celestial shimmer created by the soluble carbonates in the water. Sunrise on the lake leaves an unforgetable mind picture of dazzling red, yellow and pink upon the water.

Fall foliage on Boulder Mountain

Massacre Rocks on Snake River

World famous Balanced Rock near Castleford

City of Rocks near Almo

Craters of the Moon National Monument

Boulder Mountain in spring

Fall at Sullivan Pond near Bellevue

Big Wood River near Carey

53

Mt. Regan and Sawtooth Lake

Sheep ranch near Gimlet

Headwaters of the Salmon River

Rafting the Salmon

Salmon River Canyon near Riggins

Dawn in Stanley Basin, Sawtooth National Recreation Area

Clearing storm reflections, Palisades Reservoir

Caribou Mountain

Fall in Snake River Mountains

Little Lost Range waterfall

Stalker Creek near Elkhorn Village

Yellow-headed Blackbird, Stalker Creek

Idaho Chuckar

Sawtooth Mountains

Sawtooth Lake, Sawtooth Wilderness

East Central Idaho

The largest white water rapids in Idaho are right down river from the town of Salmon. The Salmon River (the River of No Return) amazed even Lewis and Clark.

"The water runs with great violence from one rock to the other on each side, foaming and roreing thro rocks in every direction, So as to render the passage of anything impossible," said William Clark in the diaries of the Lewis and Clark expedition.

Modern adventurers, with the help of Salmon outfitters, are better prepared for the challenge and excitement of running through those same rocks and rapids. You can shoot through Big Mallard Falls, Gunbarrel Falls and dozens of other rapid water spumes. The guides will enhance your Salmon River trip even further by stopping for exploration of sandy beaches, abandoned mines and old homesteads. Mountain wildflowers sway on the escarpments over the river in matching cadence to the waters thundering beat. Indian petroglyphs dot your passage and rare bighorn sheep may look down at you from rocky vantage points.

River trips vary from one to eight days and a variety of trips can be arranged through outfitters. Specialty outings range from fishing trips to photographic trips.

A stay in Salmon in July will insure participation in an old-fashioned parade along with plenty of other family activities.

The Middle Fork of the Salmon River is the heart of Idaho's back country. One of the major unspoiled rivers in the United States, it is an important steelhead and salmon producer and key winter range for elk, mule deer, mountain goats and bighorn sheep. The Salmon River winds through the Frank Church River of No Return Wilderness, the largest wilderness area in the U.S. south of Alaska, containing nearly 2.4 million acres. Six national forests are located within the designated wilderness.

Though the Salmon River is dramatic competition, other attractions are quite alluring. Backpackers and hikers will find hiking trails ranging from some easy walking spots to the more challenging terrain along the Continental Divide. The Salmon National Forest holds unending backpacking possibilities…hiking to a high mountain lake or walking a trail along the River of No Return. Williams Lake is another nice spot. Lakeside lodging and dining bring a little civilization back to the outdoor-oriented lifestyle.

Meadow Lake, situated in a glacial cirque valley, is one of the most beautiful recreation spots in the country. It's a high lake (9200 feet) accessible only from July through Labor Day. Mountain goats can be seen on the ridges above the lake.

Panther Creek Hot Springs (west of Salmon) spouts 180 degree water directly into Hot Springs Creek. A series of pools tempered by various amounts of hot and cold water are yours for a ten minute walk up Hot Springs Creek Road.

The heart of central Idaho belongs to the Sawtooth National Recreation Area. The jagged snow-topped peaks of the Sawtooth Mountains stretch for thirty miles in any direction. Thick forests conceal hundreds of campgrounds, many along rivers or nearby alpine lakes. If you don't stay at one of the Forest Service campsites or a private campground, the guest ranches and lodges are welcoming spots. Many of the facilities rent boats, or will set you up with a guide for trips into the wilderness. The Sawtooth area was named one of the seven most desirable places in the country for pollution-free air, water, climate, accessibility and space to breathe by the U.S. Interior Department.

The 10,000 foot Sawtooth Peaks tower over the town of Stanley on the west and south.

(Opposite) Ranchland south of Ketchum

Old homestead in Teton Valley

The town sits where tumbling Valley Creek meets the Salmon River. The White Cloud Mountains on the east, and the Salmon River Range on the north, complete the circle of mountains surrounding Stanley. Fishing, water skiing, swimming, boating, mountaineering, hiking, kayaking, snowmobiling, nordic skiing, ice fishing and reliving the past in ghost towns and museums—are all activities related to the Stanley area. Stanley is a gateway to the Sawtooth Wilderness, which is accessible only by foot or horse. The area offers 180 glacial lakes and miles of scenic trails lead through rocky canyons and forest meadows.

Seemingly worlds away from the forest setting near Stanley are the craters near the town of Arco. Along Highway 20 lies the Craters of the Moon National Monument. The desolate moonscape hides caves and craters among sharp mountains of black cinders and cones. Early pioneers made it a point to avoid the eerie landscape, but modern astronauts found it a valuable setting for moon-mission training. A visitors center offers guided tours, or you can wander on your own, using walking paths that lead to ancient rock shelters built by Indian hunting parties. A short walk to the Indian tunnel gives a chance to explore ice-lined lava tubes. Another trail leads to Great Owl Cavern.

Stunted pine grow along the trails. Some of these miniature trees are over 300 years old.

Heading down Highway 22 you'll reach the edge of the Lost River Sinks. Here, the Big and Little Lost Rivers disappear into lava beds, traveling underground for a hundred miles before reaching the Snake River near Hagerman.

Near Arco stands the world's first nuclear power plant. Arco is the first city in the world to use electricity generated by nuclear power. Fifty miles or so west of Blackfoot, Experimental Breeder Reactor #1 is now a historic landmark. By self-guided tour you'll discover how the plant operated—by touring the control room, seeing the reactor and more.

North of Arco Mt. Borah rises to 12,662 feet, claiming the title of Idaho's tallest peak. During your drive to Mt. Borah keep an eye open for wildlife. Deer and antelope may watch your passage and chipmunks, ground squirrels, and porcupines scamper about among sagebrush and pine.

The center of Fremont County is St. Anthony, also home to the head office of the Targhee National Forest. Notable sites lie within a short radius of St. Anthony. Quayle Lake is popular, as are Warm River, the Ice Caves, and Upper and Lower Mesa Falls. Mount Sawtell affords a view of three states and Yellowstone National Park. The Civil Defense Caves are relatively unexplored caves known to run at least eighteen miles; the old volcanic labyrinth was once a causeway for water, steam and lava.

Harriman State Park is a 16,000 acre wildlife refuge, historic site and working cattle ranch that offers hiking trails, wagon rides, tours of historic buildings and natural history walks.

Idaho Falls, where the wide Snake River plunges in a waterfall, is the center of antelope country. The plains wave in a patchwork of gold and green, and bees float over flowering potato fields. The state's third largest city, Idaho Falls holds all the modern amenities of shopping, excellent restaurants, good schools, and more, without sacrificing its relationship with the land—a characteristic found throughout the state of Idaho.

Idaho can be a land of sudden peaks and knife-edged ridges with sheer faces. Her whitewaters scream with raw power and winter can mean snow that hugs tight up to the edge of your windowsill. Idaho can be gentle, too, with hills that roll in lazy undulation, or she can display her sense of drama in a summer's backdrop of a dramatic sunset where the sun's departure is lauded by the song of bullfrogs. Idaho is a land of contrasts that cannot fail to please the beauty lover in all of us.

Idaho's higher reaches are not easily inhabited (though mountain goats and eagles are fond natives here), but further downslope you may find a deep blue bowl of lake lying in an alpine meadow that is surrounded by a collar of snow even in the summertime. In these meadows deer, elk, bears and coyotes roam and hundreds of other smaller animals and birds nestle among the surrounding branches or inside burrows. Idaho has a wealth of land where animals can still abide without competition from skyscrapers and freeways,

Everson Lake in the Lemhi Mountains

Pass Lake, Lemhi Range

(Opposite) Lost River Mountain Range from Mt. Borah

land that is still rugged and often sees hard winters and glorious hot summers.

The summers are a bonus, but without the deep snows of winter, life in the mountains and in the valleys below would be a struggle. The snow packs are a source of wonder even in mid-year when travelers can stop along the highway and throw snowballs—even though the thermometer may be bouncing around the 70's, 80's or even the 90's. This trickling snow melt not only keeps the highcountry meadows lush and green, but the runoff can usually be forecast in order to gauge its affect on the salmon run, river rafting expeditions, and for irrigation of some of the more arid stretches of Idaho, to cite only three of the ways the state depends on snowfall.

Not crucial to the state's economic stability, but rather to her environmental health, are these inhabitants not to be forgotten—the flowers, trees, and other vegetation that make all of Idaho so lovely to the eye. Indian paintbrush simmer on the hillsides in summertime. Contrasting with the rich scarlets to deep yellows of the Indian paintbrush are the deep blue bells of gentian and the rich purples of penstemons. Wherever your eye wanders in Idaho it can feast upon the textures and hues of nature. Even the more arid expanses of hills are becoming with their hazy blue-gray topping of sagebrush.

And we cannot forget the glacial carvings and the volcanic leavings that have littered and striated the land, leaving breathtaking scenes.

Indeed, all of Idaho continues to boast of unchanging beauty. For the most part, you don't arrive in Idaho looking for racetrack-fast action, you come instead to enjoy her scenery and quiet pace. Idahoans and tourists alike tend to gravitate towards activities that keep them close to the land—activities such as fishing, boating, cycling, or gold panning. Entire vacations can, in fact, be planned around one or more of these activities. As a tourist you can easily plan these activities yourself (with the exception of some of the river rafting expeditions that require permits) or book one of many different guided expeditions or tours.

You'll find that Idaho's favorite vacation pastimes consist of old-fashioned picnic-style fun that centers around the family. There are the obvious activities of camping around a lake, or perhaps cross-country skiing in the wintertime, but more unusual excursions, such as touring old gold mining sites and ghost towns, can prove both educational and fun. Much of this fun can be had for free or at little cost, however if you want to go more "upscale," there are plenty of resorts and four-star establishments. Don't believe that Idaho is culturally backward, either. Idaho can hold her own if you insist on more urban pastimes. Idahoans aren't lacking in sophistication, either, though the pace of life in Idaho is one of the most relaxed in the United States.

Wherever you go in Idaho, you will find this beautiful state presents herself in a sensational, romantic, melodramatic fashion. Like a song that keeps popping up under your breath, a tune you can't forget, once you have glimpsed her, Idaho stays in your subconscious until she eventually lures you back again.

Shoshone Falls near Twin Falls

Pettit Lake at sunrise

Photo Credits

DON EASTMAN - *page 2; page 46; page 47 left*

GLEN EITEMILLER - *page 63 left; page 63 right*

PHIL GOSE - *page 24; page 76*

CHARLES GURCHE - *page 6; page 7; page 28; page 32; page 38; page 39; page 51 right; page 57 right; page 58; page 65; page 80*

LELAND HOWARD - *page 29; page 59; page 60; page 61 left; page 61 right; page 69; page 72 left; page 72 right; rear cover*

K. D. LARSON - *page 17; page 42; page 43; page 47 right; page 49; page 52; page 53 left; page 53 right; page 55; page 62; page 68; page 77*

BILL & JAN MOELLER - *page 50 right*

CAROL MONTEVERDE - *page 35*

LEONARD NOLT - *page 34; page 50 left; page 51 left; page 54; page 73*

MILTON D. PATTERSON - *page 15; page 25 right*

JERRY PAVIA - *page 57 left; page 64*

GEORGE WUERTHNER - *front cover; page 10; page 11; page 14; page 20; page 21; page 25 left; page 56*

About the Author

Linda Sterling-Wanner spent twenty-eight years of her life in Idaho and says, "Idaho is as unique in her scenic splendor as she is rich in her warm, charismatic people." For Wanner, just as her comments conclude, "Idaho lures you back." Many of her vacations and holidays are spent in the state.

Wanner has twelve years of writing, advertising, and marketing experience. She has worked as an advertising consultant for a radio station and for newspapers. She has also been an advertising manager, a business editor, and a director of sales and marketing. In the past several years over 300 of her articles have seen print. She also wrote for and was the managing editor of the *Willamette Writer*, a newsletter distributed to over 650 writers, for three years.

Currently, she freelances from her home-based office. Her work includes writing advertising and brochure copy, writing product reviews, editing for two book publishers, and preparing various other written material, including novels of mystery and suspense. She has two published books.

Linda Sterling-Wanner has also served as president of Willamette Writers and has been on the board of directors of that organization for several years. "While writing occupies an enormously significant part of my life," says Wanner, "the real foundation in my life comes from my family." She and her husband and four children now live in Oregon along with "seahorses, ferrets, dogs, cats, birds and whatever other creatures we're drawn to at the moment." Wanner also loves to garden when she has time, which she says fills the spot that was vacated when she gave up skydiving.

Fall Cottonwoods, Payette National Forest

Rear Cover, Early winter on the Snake River